Reading fluency

To support children in developing fluency in their reading, give them plenty of opportunities to revisit the texts. These include:

- rereading independently
- rereading with a partner
- rereading at home
- hearing the story read to them by others as they follow the printed text.

Rereading and rehearing helps children develop automatic word recognition and gives them the models of fluent, expressive reading.

Comprehension strategies

Title	Comprehension strategy taught through these Teaching Notes				
	Prediction	Questioning	Clarifying	Summarising	Imagining
Magic Tricks	✓	✓	✓	✓	✓
Houses Then and Now	✓	✓	✓	✓	✓
E-mails Home	✓	✓	✓	✓	✓
Looking after Your Dog	✓	✓	✓	✓	✓
Public Art	✓	✓	✓	✓	✓
Wonders of the World	✓	✓	✓	✓	✓

Vocabulary and phonic opportunities

This chart shows the main words used in each book. The decodable words listed should be decoded for most children at this Stage. The tricky words are common but do not conform to the phonic rules taught up to this point – children will need support to learn and recognise them. If children struggle with one of these words you can model how to read it.

Magic Tricks	High frequency decodable words	magic, tricks, this, finger(s), spoon, wand, amaze, number, had, rubber, bottle, thumb
	High frequency tricky words	friends, your, you
Houses Then and Now	High frequency decodable words	rooms, family, old, had, has, is, bathroom(s), washing, this, bedroom, new, house, was
	High frequency tricky words	houses, built, friends, kitchen, here
E-mails Home	High frequency decodable words	I, thanks, having, trip, went, long, sand, e-mail, was
	High frequency tricky words	building(s), walk, great, all, where, morning, built, guess, palace, saw
Looking after Your Dog	High frequency decodable words	after, dog, need, dry, food, water, clean, bowl(s), shampoo, lead, wash, play, brush
	High frequency tricky words	healthy, place, hose, kennel
Public Art	High frequency decodable words	public, can, be, made, sound, graffiti, hotel, shapes, trees, toilet, lights, ice
	High frequency tricky words	art, carvings, statue(s), sculpture(s)
Wonders of the World	High frequency decodable words	very, reef, look, at, map, rock(s), deep, river(s), deepest, mountain(s)
	High frequency tricky words	where, island, glacier, world, desert, largest, waterfall

tage 5
ireflies
helma Page

Teaching Notes

Contents

Introduction

Fireflies is an exciting non-fiction series within *Oxford Reading Tree*. These books are specially designed to be used alongside the Stage 5 stories. They provide practice of reading skills in a non-fiction context whilst using the same simple, repetitive sentence structures as the *Oxford Reading Tree* stories. They also contain a selection of high frequency vocabulary. Each stage builds on the reading skills and vocabulary from previous stages, and helps children to read with growing confidence. As children read these books, they should be encouraged to read independently through: using their knowledge of letter sounds; learning to recognise high frequency words on sight; using the pictures and the sense of the text to work out new vocabulary.

To help children approach each new book in this stage with confidence, prepare the children for reading by talking about the book, asking questions and using these *Teaching Notes* and the additional *Reading Notes* in the pupil books.

Using the books

This booklet provides suggestions for using the books for guided, group and independent activities. The reading activities include ideas for developing children's *word recognition* W and *language comprehension* C skills. Within word recognition, there are ideas for helping children practise their phonic skills and knowledge, as well as helping them to tackle words that are not easy to decode phonically. The language comprehension ideas include suggestions for teaching the skills of prediction, questioning, clarifying, summarising and imagining in order to help children understand the text and the whole stories. Suggestions are also provided for speaking, listening and writing activities as well as for introducing any linked electronic material and cross-curricular links.

Curriculum coverage chart

	Speaking and listening activities	Reading	Writing
Magic Tricks			
PNS Literacy Framework (Y1)	1.3	W 5.1, 5.7 C 7.1, 7.4	10.1
National Curriculum	Working towards Level 2		
Scotland (5–14) (P2)	Level A		
N. Ireland (P2/Y2)	1, 11, 13	1, 2, 3, 6, 8, 9, 14, 15, 17	1, 3, 6, 8
Wales (Key Stage 1)	Range: 1, 2 Skills: 1, 2	Range: 1, 2, 3, 4 Skills: 1, 2	Range: 1, 3, 4 Skills: 5, 6
	Speaking and listening activities	**Reading**	**Writing**
Houses Then and Now			
PNS Literacy Framework (Y1)	3.3	W 5.6 C 7.2, 7.4	10.1
National Curriculum	Working towards Level 2		
Scotland (5–14) (P2)	Level A		
N. Ireland (P2/Y2)	1, 5, 6, 8, 10, 11	1, 2, 3, 8, 9, 14, 15, 16	6, 8
Wales (Key Stage 1)	Range: 1, 2, 3 Skills: 1, 2, 3, 4	Range: 1, 2, 3, 4 Skills: 1, 2	Range: 3, 4 Skills: 5, 6

C = Language comprehension Y = Year

W = Word recognition P = Primary

In the designations such as 1.2, the first number represents the strand and the second number the bullet point.

Curriculum coverage chart

	Speaking and listening activities	Reading	Writing
E-mails Home			
PNS Literacy Framework (Y1)	2.1	W 5.3 C 7.1, 7.2	11.1
National Curriculum	Working towards Level 2		
Scotland (5–14) (P2)	Level A		
N. Ireland (P2/Y2)	1, 6, 8, 9	1, 2, 3, 8, 9, 15, 16, 17	3, 5, 6
Wales (Key Stage 1)	Range: 1, 2, 3 Skills: 1, 2, 3, 4	Range: 1, 2, 3, 4 Skills: 1, 2	Range: 1, 3, 5 Skills: 4, 5, 6
	Speaking and listening activities	**Reading**	**Writing**
Looking after Your Dog			
PNS Literacy Framework (Y1)	3.2	W 5.5 C 7.1, 7.4	10.1
National Curriculum	Working towards Level 2		
Scotland (5–14) (P2)	Level A		
N. Ireland (P2/Y2)	1, 2, 5, 6, 9, 10	1, 2, 4, 5, 6, 8, 9, 15, 16, 17	1, 2, 3, 6, 8
Wales (Key Stage 1)	Range: 1, 2, 3 Skills: 2, 3, 4	Range: 1, 2, 3 Skills: 1, 2	Range: 1, 3, 4 Skills: 5, 6

Curriculum coverage chart

	Speaking and listening activities	Reading	Writing
Public Art			
PNS Literacy Framework (Y1)	3.3	W 5.4 C 7.2, 8.3	9.2
National Curriculum	Working towards Level 2		
Scotland (5–14) (P2)	Level A		
N. Ireland (P2/Y2)	1, 5, 6, 8, 9, 10	1, 2, 3, 8, 9, 14	1, 3, 5, 6
Wales (Key Stage 1)	Range: 1, 2, 3 Skills: 1, 2, 3, 4	Range: 1, 2, 3, 4 Skills: 1, 2	Range: 3, 4 Skills: 3, 4, 5
	Speaking and listening activities	**Reading**	**Writing**
Wonders of the World			
PNS Literacy Framework (Y1)	1.4	W 5.3 C 7.1, 7.4	11.1, 11.2
National Curriculum	Working within Level 2		
Scotland (5–14) (P2)	Level A		
N. Ireland (P2/Y2)	1, 6, 8, 9, 10	1, 2, 3, 7, 8, 9, 15, 16, 17	1, 6, 8
Wales (Key Stage 1)	Range: 1, 2, 3 Skills: 2, 3, 4	Range: 1, 2, 3 Skills: 1, 2	Range: 1, 3, 4 Skills: 3, 5, 7

Magic Tricks

C = Language comprehension *R, AF* = QCA Reading assessment focus
W = Word recognition *W, AF* = QCA Writing assessment focus

Group or guided reading

Introducing the book

C *(Clarifying)* Look carefully at the front and back covers and ask the children to say whether this is a story or an information book. Remind children of the terms 'fiction' and 'non-fiction'.

C *(Prediction)* Ask the children to say what they think they will find out from this book.

Strategy check

Find the word 'magic' on page 3, then find the word 'magician'. Notice which letters are the same in both words. Read both words. Find 'Squeeze' on page 12. Use phonemes to work out this word together. Remind the children to look carefully at words and use the letter sounds when working out new words.

Independent reading

- Ask children to read the book aloud. Praise and encourage them while they read, and prompt as necessary.

C *(Summarising, Clarifying)* Ask children to say which trick they would like to try and explain why.

Assessment Check that children:

- *(R, AF1)* keep their place on the page either by pointing to words or to lines of text
- *(R, AF1)* use phonic knowledge and the context to work out new words
- *(R, AF2)* can follow the sequence of instructions and understand how each trick works.

Returning to the text

C *(Prediction)* On pages 4 and 5, ask the children to say what they think will happen in each of these tricks.

C *(Imagining)* On page 6, read the title of the trick and ask: *Can you think of another way that you could make a spoon stick to your fingers?*

C *(Questioning)* Look at the picture on page 21 and ask: *Why did the stick not fall out of the bottle?*

Group and independent reading activities

Objective Find specific information in simple texts (7.1).

C *(Questioning)* Look at the contents list on page 2 and the index on page 24. Ask: *What is the difference between a contents list and an index?* Notice that the contents page lists the chapters of the book in the order they come in the book, and that the index lists words from the text in alphabetical order.

- Choose one of the tricks, e.g. Trick Two. Ask the children to tell you the page number where you can begin reading. Find the page and reread this trick.
- Then choose a word from the index, e.g. magician. Ask the children to tell you the page number where this word can be found. Turn to the page and find the word. Ask the children to suggest other words or headings that can be found by looking in the contents or in the index.

Assessment *(R, AF2)* Could the children use the contents and the index pages to find particular information?

Objective Recognise the main elements that shape different texts (7.4).

C *(Clarifying, Questioning, Imagining)* Ask the children to tell you what they know about writing instructions. Make a list of their suggestions. Remind them that they need a title, a list of things you need and sentences telling you what to do in the right order.

- Look at Trick Two and ask: *What is the title? What do you need? What do you do first?* Find and read all the instruction words: Ask, Tell, Hold, Squeeze, etc. Read instructions 1 and 2 together, then turn the page and read instructions 4 and 5, missing number 3. Ask: *Will the trick still work? What will happen?* Talk about the need to follow instructions carefully to make sure things will work.

Assessment *(R, AF2)* Did the children understand the main elements of the instructions? Did they understand the effect of missing out an instruction?

Objective Read and spell phonically decodable two-syllable and three-syllable words (5.7).
Recognise and use alternative ways of pronouncing graphemes already taught (5.1).

W Make a list of these words from the book: magic, finger, sticking, number, pencil, empty, without, together. Read each word in turn, counting and clapping the syllables. Go back to 'magic'. Say the syllables: ma/gic. Say the phonemes in each syllable. Notice the sound of 'g' in this word. Spell the word using letter sounds, then using letter names. Repeat this for each word in the list. When you spell 'pencil' notice the soft sound of 'c' in this word compared with the hard sound in 'magic'. Cover the words and ask the children to attempt spelling them without help.

Assessment *(R, AF1)* Could the children identify syllables in words? Could they identify the phonemes in each syllable and spell the words?

E-links

E-Fireflies

This book is available electronically, on *e-Fireflies* Stages 3–6 CD-ROM. You can read the text as a 'Talking Book' on a whiteboard with the whole class, or on a computer with a group of children. Use the tools to annotate the text with the children. The children can then use 'Make a Book' to select their own choice of content and make their own books. Use the Teacher Settings screen to select how you want any part of the CD-ROM to be used, and the Progress Report Chart to track the progress of individual children.

Speaking and listening activities

Objective Interpret a text by reading aloud with some variety in pace and emphasis (1.3).

Ask individuals to read the instructions for one of the tricks to the rest of the group. Praise them for reading fluently, keeping everyone's attention and for reading with expression. Notice exclamation marks and help the children to read with appropriate emphasis.

Cross-curricular links: National Curriculum Key Stage 1

ICT

Pupils should be taught:

- How to plan and give instructions to make things happen.

Writing activities

Objective Write chronological texts using simple structures (10.1).

Talk about Trick Two. Ask the children to explain how the number gets onto the friend's hand. Talk through the sequence of events: write on the sugar cube, press on your thumb, press on your friend's hand.

- Ask the children to write three or four sentences explaining how the number gets on the friend's hand. Use sentence beginnings that show an order of events: 'First your friend writes a number on a sugar cube. Then… After that… Finally...'

Assessment *(W, AF2)* Were the children able to put the events in order and write sentences explaining what happened?

Houses Then and Now

C = Language comprehension — *R, AF* = QCA Reading assessment focus
W = Word recognition — *W, AF* = QCA Writing assessment focus

Group or guided reading

Introducing the book

C *(Clarifying)* Look at the front cover and read the title. Notice where the words 'Then' and 'Now' are placed. Ask the children to explain why this is so.

C *(Prediction)* Read the blurb and look at the pictures on the back cover. Ask the children to say what they think the book will be about.

C *(Clarifying)* Look at some of the pictures and ask the children to explain how they know that this is a non-fiction book. Ask: *How would a story book be different?*

Strategy check

Look at the contents page together. Read the headings. Remind the children that they will find the information in this order in the book.

Independent reading

- Ask the children to read the book aloud. Praise and encourage them while they read, and prompt as necessary.

C *(Summarising)* Ask the children to say what they think is the biggest change between a modern house and a 100-year-old house.

Assessment Check that children:

- *(R, AF1)* know how to keep their place in the text with a bookmark, or by following the text with a finger
- *(R, AF1)* use phonic knowledge and the context to work out new words
- *(R, AF2)* can talk about the changes in homes shown in the book.

Returning to the text

C *(Imagining)* Ask the children to say what the changes will be one hundred years from now. Ask: *What do you think might be different in the future?*

C *(Clarifying)* Ask the children about the new house. Ask: *Is your house like this? In what ways is it different? How is your house different from the old house?*

C *(Questioning)* Ask: *How did people use to wash themselves? Did they have showers? What did they have instead?* Ask the children to tell you the page number that gives the answer.

Group and independent reading activities

Objective Use syntax and context when reading for meaning (7.2).

C *(Questioning)* Ask the children to find the word 'parlour' on page 4. Ask: *Can you explain what a parlour was?* Ask the children to find a sentence on page 4 that tells us about the parlour. Ask the children if they have a similar room in their own home.

- Find 'larder' on page 13. Ask the children to tell you what they have found out about a larder. Ask: *What do we usually use instead of a larder?*

Assessment *(R, AF2)* Did the children use the context to work out the meaning of the new words?

Objective Recognise the main elements that shape different texts (7.4).

C *(Clarifying, Questioning)* Read the contents list on page 2 together. Notice that the Old House is on page 3, and the New House is on page 6. Ask: *What do you think is on pages 4 and 5?* Look at pages 4 and 5 to find out if the children are right. Go back to the contents page and ask: *How many pages are about bathrooms?* Agree that information about bathrooms is on pages 8, 9, 10 and 11. Turn to those pages to check. Choose one of the headings from the contents page to read about. Turn to that page and read it. Notice that information on the same topic continues until a new heading appears.

Assessment *(R, AF2)* Did the children understand that the page listed for a heading in the contents was on ly the first page of that information, and they could find out more by turning the pages until they reached a new heading?

Objective Read more challenging texts that can be decoded using their acquired phonic knowledge and skills, along with automatic recognition of high frequency words (5.6).

- (W) Using the high frequency words from the chart on page 4, make a list or set of flash cards to make sure that the children can recognise these words on sight.
- Ask the children to find long or unfamiliar words in the book. Talk about ways to work out these words: using syllables, using letter sounds, using the sense of the sentence and the picture. Take turns to read aloud from the book. Praise the children for working out new words independently.

Assessment *(R, AF1)* Could the children use their knowledge of phonics, word structure and sight vocabulary to read with confidence?

E-links

Fireflies Plus

If you are an Espresso user, you can access cross-curricular videos and multimedia activities (including writing opportunities and quizzes) linked to this title to enrich your children's reading. Children can also write, post and compare reviews of the book. Full supporting Teaching Notes for this content are available on the site in PDF format. Within the Espresso site, follow the route **<Channel guide → English 1 → Oxford Reading Tree Fireflies Plus logo>.** *Espresso Primary* is an extensive library of cross-curricular, video-rich broadband teaching resources and learning activities that motivates children and supports teachers.

Speaking and listening activities

Objective Explain their views to others in a small group, decide how to report the group's views to the class (3.3).

Divide the children into groups and ask them to think of four important things to have in a house. You could start with 'Somewhere to cook food'. Ask the children to think of three more. Ask one person from each group to share their ideas with the class. Praise children for speaking clearly and for sensible answers.

Cross-curricular links: National Curriculum Key Stage 1

History

Pupils should be taught to:

- Identify differences between ways of life at different times.

Writing activities

Objective Write non-chronological texts using simple structures (10.1).

Provide a piece of paper for each child with space for eight pictures. Look at pages 22 and 23. Talk about the first picture on page 23, ask the children to draw their own home in the first space on their sheet. Ask the children to identify each picture on page 23, then draw a picture of that place in their own home. Ask them to write a simple caption for each picture, e.g. my home, my lounge, etc. Use page 22 and the children's pictures to make your own Then and Now display.

Assessment *(W, AF2)* Could the children replace the pictures in the book with pictures of their own homes?

E-mails Home

C = Language comprehension	*R, AF* = QCA Reading assessment focus
W = Word recognition	*W, AF* = QCA Writing assessment focus

Group or guided reading

Introducing the book

C *(Clarifying)* Read the title and look at the picture. Ask the children to say what they know about e-mails. Look at the row of icons along the top of the page. Explain, or ask one of the children to explain, the Internet and the meaning of each little picture.

C *(Prediction)* Read the blurb on the back cover and look at the picture. Ask the children to explain what they think the book will be about.

Strategy check

Read the list of words on the back cover and the words listed for long vowel sounds. Remind the children to use their knowledge of phonics to help work out new words.

Independent reading

- Ask children to read the book aloud. Praise and encourage them while they read, and prompt as necessary.

C *(Summarising, Questioning)* Ask children to tell you who the boy was sending e-mails to. Ask: *Why did he send e-mails home?*

Assessment Check that children:

- *(R, AF1)* point as they read, or keep their place with a bookmark under the line of text
- *(R, AF1)* use phonic knowledge and the context to work out new words
- *(R, AF2)* understand that these are messages to a friend at home.

Returning to the text

C *(Questioning)* Ask the children to use the index on page 24 to find out about particular subjects or places, e.g. ask: *Can you find out about sand dunes? Which pages tell us about London?*

- C *(Imagining)* Ask the children to think of any place they know well. Ask them to say what clues they could give to help people guess the location.
- C *(Clarifying)* Ask: *Which of the places in the book would you like to visit? Why?*

Group and independent reading activities

Objective Find specific information in simple texts (7.1).

- C *(Questioning)* Ask the children to find a question in the text on page 5. Read all the text on the double page but do not turn the page to get the answer. Ask the children to find clues to the place in the sentences. Ask them to tell you what clues they can find in the pictures. If they can answer the question, ask them to tell you the piece of information that was most useful.
- Repeat with the questions on pages 11, 17 and 23. Ask: *On which pages were the pictures most helpful in guessing the location? On which pages were the sentences most helpful?*

Assessment *(R, AF2)* Could the children find clues to the location in the text? Could they find clues in the pictures?

Objective Use syntax and context when reading for meaning (7.2).

- C *(Prediction, Clarifying)* Cover these words in the text with sticky notes: buildings (twice on page 4), Australia (page 6), enemies (page 13), palace (page 22).
- Read the book together. When you reach a covered word ask the children to suggest a word that would make sense. Encourage them to reread the whole page and look carefully at the picture. When they have made some suggestions, peel back the paper slowly to reveal one letter at a time. Check that your prediction was correct. Repeat with the remaining words. Praise children for making sensible predictions.

Assessment *(R, AF2)* Could the children use the sense of the sentence and the syntax to predict words correctly?

Objective Identify the constituent parts of two-syllable and three-syllable words to support the application of phonic knowledge and skills (5.3).

W Find some two-syllable words in the text ending in –ing: building, having, morning. Ask the children to say the syllables separately: build/ing, hav/ing, morn/ing. Look carefully at 'building' before attempting to spell the word.

- Ask the children to make these words into –ing words: march, fly, walk, fall, blow. Help them to use syllables to spell the words correctly. Ask the children to say the syllables and tell you the letters to write as you make a list of –ing words.

Assessment *(R, AF1)* Could the children identify syllables in these words? Did they understand that syllables help us to read and spell words?

Speaking and listening activities

Objective Listen with sustained concentration, building new stores of words in different contexts (2.1).

Give one child the book and ask them to open it at random. Ask them to give clues to a place without naming it, e.g. use pages 18 and 19 to say: 'This place is in Southern Africa. It has many sand dunes'. When everyone has had a chance to guess the name of the place, pass the book to someone else to open and read different clues. Praise children for giving clues without naming the place.

Cross-curricular links: National Curriculum Key Stage 1

ICT

Pupils should be taught the knowledge, skills and understanding through:

- Exploring a variety of ICT tools.
- Talking about the use of ICT inside and outside school.

Geography

Pupils should be taught to:

- Identify and describe what places are like.

Writing activities

Objective Compose and write simple sentences independently to communicate meaning (11.1).

Use e-mail on the school computer. Ask the children to take turns to write a simple message to a friend, using the class e-mail address. They can write about anything they like. Send messages, then make time for children to open messages they receive and read them to the class.

Assessment *(W, AF2)* Were the children able to write sentences on a topic of their own choice?

Looking after Your Dog

C = Language comprehension	*R, AF* = QCA Reading assessment focus
W = Word recognition	*W, AF* = QCA Writing assessment focus

Group or guided reading

Introducing the book

C *(Prediction)* Read the title and ask the children to say what they think this book will be about.

C *(Clarifying)* Read the blurb on the back cover. Ask: *What else does a dog need, apart from food, play and keeping clean?* Praise children for making sensible suggestions.

Strategy check

Remind children to use the sense of the sentence and letter sounds to work out new words.

Independent reading

- Ask children to read the book aloud. Praise and encourage them while they read, and prompt as necessary.

C *(Summarising, Questioning)* Ask children to tell you from memory some of the things a dog needs. Use the book afterwards to check for anything they missed.

Assessment Check that children:

- *(R, AF1)* point as they read, or keep their place with a bookmark under the line of text
- *(R, AF1)* use phonic knowledge and the context to work out new words
- *(R, AF2)* can talk about the basic needs of a dog.

Returning to the text

C *(Questioning)* Ask: *What did you find out about washing a dog? What would you need? Why do we need to wash a dog?*

C *(Imagining)* Ask the children to imagine the kind of dog they would most like to have as a pet. Ask them to describe the dog and say what they would call it.

C *(Summarising)* Ask: *If you have a dog, what do have to remember to do every day?*

Group and independent reading activities

Objective Find specific information in simple texts (7.1).

C *(Summarising, Clarifying)* Ask the children to show you pages where there is a word in red (pages 11, 13, 16 and 18). Ask: *Why is this word in red? What does red on notices usually mean?* Read the sentences following 'Remember' and ask: *Why is it important to remember these things?* Agree that they are all advice and warnings, so we must notice these sentences in particular.

- Ask: *Can you think of a 'Remember' warning that could go on page 8?* (e.g. Remember that your dog will drink a lot more water in hot weather.) Ask children to explain why it was a good idea to write 'Remember' in red.

Assessment *(R, AF2)* Could the children find the 'Remember' sentences and understand why they were important messages?

Objective Recognise the main elements that shape different texts (7.4).

C *(Questioning, Clarifying)* Read the introduction together, and ask children to explain what an introduction is for. Read page 5 and ask: *Is this a page of instructions, or is it an explanation?* Read the page together and agree that it is explaining why dogs need food.

- Ask the children to say how they recognise instructions. Ask them to find a page where instructions begin. Notice the 'You will need' and 'What to do' headings.
- Then read the first word in each sentence on page 7. Ask: *What do you notice about these words?* (They all tell us what to do; they are commands.) Ask the children to find some more command words in the book. Make a list. Ask the children to tell you how they will

recognise instruction texts. (What you need; What to do headings; command words at the beginning of sentences.)

Assessment *(R, AF2)* Could the children identify instruction texts? Did they understand the main features of instructions?

Objective Apply phonic knowledge and skills as the prime approach to reading and spelling unfamiliar words that are not completely decodable (5.5).

- W Write words from the book that are not completely decodable on the board, e.g. healthy, biscuits, young. Look at each word in turn. Say the letter sounds in the order they appear in the word, e.g. h–ea–l–th–y. Say the word as it sounds, then read the whole sentence (e.g. on page 4) again and say the word that makes sense. Look again at the word to see which letters do not sound in the word. Practise spelling the word.
- Repeat with the other words. Praise children for using both phonics and the context to read unfamiliar words.

Assessment *(R, AF1)* Could the children use their phonic knowledge to work out new words? Could they spell the new words?

E-links

E-Fireflies

This book is available electronically, on *e-Fireflies* Stages 3–6 CD-ROM. You can read the text as a 'Talking Book' on a whiteboard with the whole class, or on a computer with a group of children. Use the tools to annotate the text with the children. The children can then use 'Make a Book' to select their own choice of content and make their own books. Use the Teacher Settings screen to select how you want any part of the CD-ROM to be used, and the Progress Report Chart to track the progress of individual children.

Speaking and listening activities

Objective Ask and answer questions, make relevant contributions, offer suggestions and take turns (3.2).

Ask children to work in groups of four. Ask them to choose a pet that they know about. Ask them each to think of a different thing that the pet needs. They practise saying their sentence to each other, then groups take turns to report back to the whole class.

Cross-curricular links: National Curriculum Key Stage 1

Sc 2 Science

Pupils should be taught:

- That humans and other animals need food and water to stay alive.
- How to treat animals with care and sensitivity.

Writing activities

Objective Write non-chronological texts using simple structures (10.1).

Ask children to work in pairs and choose a pet they know about. Ask them to choose one set of instructions from the book, then change the instructions to suit a different pet, e.g. change the kennel to a hutch, or a cage. Ask them to work together to write a 'You will need' list and 'What to do' instructions for the pet they have chosen.

Assessment *(W, AF2)* Were the children able to write instructions using the book as a prompt?

Public Art

C = Language comprehension — R, AF = QCA Reading assessment focus
W = Word recognition — W, AF = QCA Writing assessment focus

Group or guided reading

Introducing the book

C *(Prediction)* Look at the picture on the front cover and ask: *Where do you think this painting is? Is it indoors or outdoors?* Read the title and talk about the word 'public' as opposed to 'private'.

C *(Clarifying)* Read the blurb on the back cover. Ask the children to tell you about any art that can be looked at in public near where you live. Talk about any murals or sculptures in the school grounds.

Strategy check

Remind the children that non-fiction books do not always have to be read in order. They can choose subjects from the contents list after reading the introduction. Ask them to tell you how they will tackle unfamiliar words.

Independent reading

- Ask children to read the book aloud. Praise and encourage them while they read, and prompt as necessary.

C *(Summarising, Clarifying)* Ask children to show you the pages that they found most interesting. Ask: *What interested you about these pages?*

Assessment Check that children:

- *(R, AF1)* keep their place as they read, either by pointing to the words or by using a bookmark under a line of text
- *(R, AF1)* use phonic knowledge and the context to work out new words
- *(R, AF2)* can talk about the different kinds of art and express opinions about them.

Returning to the text

C *(Questioning)* Ask: *What did you find out about the Ice Hotel? Where is it? What is special about it?* Ask the children to find the pages and show you where the answers are.

C *(Imagining)* Look at Ice Carving on page 14 and Sand Sculptures on pages 20 and 21. Ask the children to imagine which is more difficult to carve. Ask: *What would be the problems with carving ice? What would be the problems with carving sand?*

C *(Questioning)* Ask: *What was special about the Colourful Toilet? Did you like it?*

Group and independent reading activities

Objective Use syntax and context when reading for meaning (7.2).

C *(Questioning)* Ask: *Have you heard the word 'definition'?* Explain that a definition tells us what words mean. Turn to page 3. Read the sentences together. Ask: *What does the book say that public art is?* Point out that the second sentence gives a definition of 'public art'.

- Turn to page 22 and read all the text together. Ask children to find the sentence 'This is called graffiti'. Ask them to find the answer to the question, 'What is called graffiti?' Praise them for finding the answer in the first sentence.
- Turn to page 14. Read the text and the caption for the photograph. Ask the children to use this information to make up a definition of 'Ice Sculpture'.

Assessment *(R, AF2)* Did the children understand that meanings of new words can be found in the text? Could they find definitions in the text? Could they use information to form a definition?

Objective Distinguish fiction and non-fiction texts and the different purposes for reading them (8.3).

C *(Clarifying, Imagining)* Ask the children to tell you the meanings of the words 'fiction' and 'non-fiction'. Ask: *When do you choose a non-fiction book? When do you choose a story?* Ask: *When you pick up a book, how can you tell the difference?* Talk about the title, blurb, use of photographs and diagrams, contents and index pages. Ask them to tell you the clues that would tell them that 'Public Art' is a non-fiction book.

- Suggest instead that the cover is the picture of a story book called 'Public Art'. Look at the children on the cover. Ask: *Who might be the main characters?* Discuss what might happen in the story. Ask: *Where might this wall be? Whose idea was it to paint it? Will adults be pleased with the children, or cross?*

Assessment *(R, AF2)* Could the children say how they recognise fact and fiction books? Could they contribute ideas for a story based on the cover picture?

Objective Recognise automatically an increasing number of familiar high frequency words (5.4).

W Use the list of high frequency words listed in the table on page 4. Choose particular words to practise, e.g. could (page 15), people (page 22), night (page 12). Find and read each word in the text. Read the whole sentence each time. Select words that children are finding difficult to remember. Make a set of cards showing the words. Play flashcard games and word matching games.

Assessment *(R, AF1)* Could the children recognise the high frequency words on sight?

E-links

Fireflies Plus

If you are an Espresso user, you can access cross-curricular videos and multimedia activities (including writing opportunities and quizzes) linked to this title to enrich your children's reading. Children can also write, post and compare reviews of the book. Full supporting Teaching Notes for this content are available on the site in PDF format. Within the Espresso site, follow the route **<Channel guide → English 1 → Oxford Reading Tree Fireflies Plus logo>.** *Espresso Primary* is an extensive library of cross-curricular, video-rich broadband teaching resources and learning activities that motivates children and supports teachers.

Speaking and listening activities

Objective Explain their views to others in a small group, decide how to report the group's views to the class (3.3).

Ask the children to work in groups of three or four. Ask them to think about the school grounds and decide if there is a wall that would look better if it had a mural. Ask: *What would the mural show? Is there a space that would look better with a piece of sculpture? What would the sculpture be?* Remind them to listen to each other's ideas and to think of reasons for their choices. Ask groups, in turn, to tell the rest of the class what they have decided.

Cross-curricular links: National Curriculum Key Stage 1

Art and Design

Children should be taught about:

- Materials and processes used in making art, craft and design.

Writing activities

Objective Use key features of narrative in their own writing (9.2).

Use the ideas generated from the group reading activity on fiction and non-fiction books. Remind the children of the main points. Write a list of the main ideas. Ask the children to work alone or in pairs to make up and write a story about the children on the cover of the book, and why they decided to paint this wall.

Assessment *(W, AF2)* Were the children able to write a short story about the cover picture?

Wonders of the World

C = Language comprehension — *R, AF* = QCA Reading assessment focus
W = Word recognition — *W, AF* = QCA Writing assessment focus

Group or guided reading

Introducing the book

C *(Prediction)* Look at the four pictures on the front cover and ask the children to say what they think they show. Read the title and ask: *What kind of wonders do you think this book will be about?*

C *(Clarifying)* Look at some of the pictures and ask the children to say what kind of wonders these are. Match the pictures on the cover to pictures in the book and identify each photograph.

Strategy check

Read the heading on page 4. Find the same words in the caption and notice the arrow showing the location. Find the same words again in the text. Remind children to use their knowledge of letter sounds to work out the names of the locations in the book.

Independent reading

- Ask children to read the book aloud. Praise and encourage them while they read, and prompt as necessary.

C *(Summarising, Clarifying)* Look at the contents list on page 1. Ask the children to tell you which wonder interested them most. Read the pages again and ask the children to say why they chose those pages.

Assessment Check that children:

- *(R, AF1)* point as they read or use a bookmark to keep their place
- *(R, AF1)* use phonic knowledge and the context to work out new words
- *(R, AF2)* understand why each feature has been chosen as a wonder of the world.

Returning to the text

- C *(Questioning)* Ask the children to use the contents page to find the page numbers for the highest mountain and the biggest desert. Praise them for locating these pages correctly.
- C *(Summarising, Clarifying)* Ask: *Why are there maps in this book? How do the maps help us understand the information in the text?*
- C *(Imagining, Clarifying)* Ask the children to think of an animal that could be included as a 'Wonder of the Animal World'. Ask them to suggest an animal and say why they think it would be a wonder.

Group and independent reading activities

Objective Find specific information in simple texts (7.1).

- C *(Questioning)* Find the glossary on page 24. Tell the children that a glossary lists important words in this book and explains what each word means. Ask them to find the word 'glacier' in the list and read the meaning. Then find the word 'Glacier' in the contents page. Read pages 8 and 9 again.
- Find 'canyon' in the glossary and in the contents. Ask children to tell you where you will find out more about a canyon. Praise them for finding the right page in the book. Read pages 18 and 19 again.
- Finally find 'desert' in the glossary, in the contents and read pages 14 and 15.

Assessment *(R, AF2)* Could the children find the words in the glossary and read the definitions? Could they use the contents page to find the relevant part of the book?

Objective Recognise the main elements that shape different texts (7.4).

- C *(Clarifying, Summarising)* Ask the children to tell you the features that show this is a non-fiction book, e.g. maps, photographs, headings, a glossary. Ask: *Can you read this book in any order, or does it only make sense if you start at the beginning and read every page?* Talk about using the contents list to find items of interest and notice that you can read about them in any order.

- Turn to page 13 and ask: *Why is a photograph better than a drawing of a waterfall? What does the photograph show us?* Look at the map on page 12 and ask: *What information does this map give us? Does it tell us more than the text? How does it help us understand about Angel Falls?* Look at photographs and maps on other pages and notice the additional information they provide.

Assessment *(R, AF2)* Could the children explain why maps and photographs help us understand the information in this book?

Objective Identify the constituent parts of two-syllable and three-syllable words to support the application of phonic knowledge and skills (5.3).

W Look for words in the book that have three syllables: animals, glacier, waterfall, submarine. Ask the children to tell you the syllables of each word and write it showing the separations: an–im–als, gla–ci–er, etc. Say all the phonemes of each syllable. Practise blending the words, then ask the children to use syllables to attempt to spell the words orally.

Assessment *(R, AF1)* Could the children identify syllables in words? Did they understand that syllables help us to read and spell words?

Speaking and listening activities

Objective Experiment with and build new stores of words to communicate in different contexts (1.4).

Use the contents page to remind children of the wonders described in the book. Ask them why a particular mountain, glacier or cave was in the book. Look at the page in the book if necessary.

- Create a list of superlatives: longest, tallest, deepest, highest, etc. Ask children to use a word from the list to tell you about a place they have been to, e.g. The highest place I have been to… The longest journey I went on… The biggest animal I have seen… The deepest water I have been in… Ask the children to think of some more words ending in –est, e.g. hottest, coldest, fastest, etc. Use these words in a similar way.

Cross-curricular links: National Curriculum Key Stage 1

Geography

Pupils should be taught to:

- Use globes, maps and plans at a range of scales.

Writing activities

Objective Compose and write simple sentences independently to communicate meaning (11.1).
Use capital letters and full stops when punctuating simple sentences (11.2).

Ask the children to tell you words that begin questions, e.g. what, where, how, when, etc. Make a list of question words. Ask each child to write a question that can be answered in this book. Remind them to use a capital letter at the beginning and a question mark at the end. Collect all the questions. Read out the questions as a quiz, giving children time to use the book to find the answers. Display all the questions and answers around a map of the world.

Assessment *(W, AF2)* Were the children able to write an appropriate question and use punctuation?

Oxford Reading Tree resources at this level

Biff, Chip and Kipper
Stage 5 Stories
Stage 5 More Stories A
Stage 5 More Stories B
Stage 5 More Stories C

Phonics
Stage 5 Songbirds

Poetry
Glow-worms Stage 5–6

Non-fiction
Stage 5 Fireflies
Stage 5 More Fireflies

Wider reading
Stage 5 Snapdragons

Electronic
Stage 5 Talking Stories
Stage 5 for Clicker
eSongbirds
eFireflies
MagicPage
Clip Art
ORT Online www.OxfordReadingTree.com

Teachers' Resources
Sequencing Cards
Comprehension Photocopy Masters (Stages 3–5)
Context Cards
Teacher's Handbook (Stages 1–9)
Stage 5 Workbooks
Stage 5 Storytape
Songbirds Teaching Notes, Guided Reading Cards and Parent Notes
Snapdragons Teaching Notes, Guided Reading Cards and Parent Notes
Fireflies Teaching Notes

OXFORD
UNIVERSITY PRESS

Great Clarendon Street, Oxford OX2 6DP

Oxford University Press is a department of the University of Oxford. It furthers the University's objective of excellence in research, scholarship, and education by publishing worldwide in

Oxford New York
Auckland Cape Town Dar es Salaam Hong Kong Karachi Kuala Lumpur Madrid Melbourne Mexico City Nairobi New Delhi Shanghai Taipei Toronto

With offices in

Argentina Austria Brazil Chile Czech Republic France Greece Guatemala Hungary Italy Japan Poland Portugal Singapore South Korea Switzerland Thailand Turkey Ukraine Vietnam

Written by Thelma Page

The moral rights of the author have been asserted

Database right Oxford University Press (maker)

First published 2008

British Library Cataloguing in Publication Data

Data available

ISBN 978-0-19-847296-4

10 9 8 7 6 5 4 3

Page make-up by Thomson Digital

Printed in China by Imago

Paper used in the production of this book is a natural, recyclable product made from wood grown in sustainable forests. The manufacturing process conforms to the environmental regulations of the country of origin.